# PLANET FOOTBALL

# GREATEST PLAYERS

# CONTENTS

Published in paperback
in 2017 by Wayland
Copyright © Hodder and
Stoughton Limited, 2017
All rights reserved
Editor: Victoria Brooker
Produced for Wayland by
Tall Tree Ltd
Designer: Gary Hyde
Editor: Jon Richards

Dewey number: 796.3'34'0922-
dc23
ISBN 978 1 5263 0127 7

Wayland, an imprint of
Hachette Children's Group
Part of Hodder and Stoughton
Carmelite House
50 Victoria Embankment
London EC4Y 0DZ
An Hachette UK Company
www.hachette.co.uk
www.hachettechildrens.co.uk

FSC

Printed and bound in China
10 9 8 7 6 5 4 3 2 1

# PLAYERS AND POSITIONS

Top footballers need to be good at the basic skills of the game as well as being excellent athletes, able to run hard and compete all game long. The world's greatest players have a little something extra which makes them stand out from the crowd and shine as match winners.

Some great players like Cristiano Ronaldo and Sergio Aguero are renowned for their goalscoring. Others, such as Lionel Messi, have great close control skills and can dribble through defences, or use their strength, like Yaya Toure, to dominate opponents. Many great players have terrific awareness of the game around them. They know where teammates and opponents are without looking, and choose the right pass or move to make.

PEPE

WOJCIECH SZCZESNY

Playing for Arsenal, Wojciech Szczesny reaches with both hands to make a terrific save and deny the New York Red Bulls from scoring.

Talent rarely succeeds on its own and the world's greatest players dedicate themselves to working hard in training and improving their skills throughout their careers. Many great players are also mentally tough. They can pick themselves up after defeats or a period of poor form, or be sharp and ready for action when they come off the bench as a substitute during a game.

**LIONEL MESSI**

**NUMBERS GAME**

**23**

The number of seconds Sergio Aguero was on the pitch as a substitute before scoring a goal against Liverpool in 2014.

**ZLATAN IBRAHIMOVIC**

Lionel Messi of Barcelona races past Pepe of Real Madrid in a clash between Spain's two dominant teams.

Star Swedish striker, Zlatan Ibrahimovic, is his country's leading goalscorer with 54 goals. He has notched up over 340 goals for his clubs, which have included Barcelona, Juventus and Paris St Germain.

5

# GOALKEEPING

The goalkeeper, or goalie, is the last line of defence, stopping shots and headers directed towards goal, sometimes with spectacular saves. A good goalie, though, must also command their penalty area and tell defenders what to do.

 HOPE SOLO

The best goalies will make sure they have an excellent view of the game, paying close attention to the match, even if play is up the other end of the pitch. They have to stay alert as the ball could head their way in the blink of an eye, forcing them to slow down an opposition attack or pull off that all-important save.

Hope Solo made her debut for the US national team in 2000. She has won two Olympic gold medals, was voted the best goalkeeper at the 2015 Women's World Cup and currently plays in the American W-League for Seattle Reign.

NUMBERS GAME

**89**

The number of clean sheets Hope Solo has had as the US team's goalkeeper.

Top goalkeepers, like Iker Casillas, put in hours of practice, saving shots from all different heights and angles. The vast majority of saves do not require spectacular diving. Instead, they rely on good footwork to form a barrier between the ball and the goal.

## FOOTBALL ICONS

NAME: .................. DINO ZOFF

NATIONALITY: ......... ITALIAN

DATE OF BIRTH: ...... 28/02/42

INTERNATIONAL CAPS: ... 112

A goalkeeper of outstanding ability, Zoff was captain of his national side and, in Spain in 1982, he became the oldest player to win the World Cup at the age of 40. He also holds the record for the longest playing time without letting in a goal – 1,142 minutes!

### IKER CASILLAS

While playing for Real Madrid and Spain, Iker Casillas won five Spanish La Liga titles, three Champions League medals, two European Championships and the 2010 FIFA World Cup.

# GOALIE SKILLS

Goalkeepers need a range of skills besides confident handling and the ability to make spectacular saves. Top keepers also need to be brave to dive at the feet of opponents or to leap high in a crowded area.

THIBAUT COURTOIS

Some modern goalkeepers, such as 1.99-m (6.5-ft) tall Thibaut Courtois, use their body size well to try to dominate when the ball comes into their penalty area. This can involve catching a high ball crossed into the box or rushing out to stop an opposing attacker who has broken through the defence with the ball.

NUMBERS GAME

16

Thibaut Courtois' age when he made his debut for top Belgian side, Genk in 2009.

Thibaut Courtois played over 100 times for Atlético Madrid before becoming the Chelsea number one keeper at the age of 22. He already has 25 caps for Belgium with whom he reached the quarter finals of the 2014 World Cup.

Sharp reactions, bravery and quick hands mark David De Gea out as one of the world's best young keepers. He was voted Manchester United's player of the year for the 2013–14 season.

Goalkeepers need to be able to kick well under pressure in order to clear the ball passed back to them by a teammate. They also need to make quick decisions when the ball is in their hands, throwing the ball out to a teammate or kicking the ball out of the hand upfield.

DAVID DE GEA

## FOOTBALL ICONS

NAME: ..... PETER SCHMEICHEL
NATIONALITY: ............ DANISH
DATE OF BIRTH: .... 18/11/1963
INTERNATIONAL CAPS: ..... 129

Manchester United got a bargain when they bought the imposing keeper from Brondby in 1991 for just £550,000. He won five Premier Leagues and the UEFA Champions League with Manchester United as well as the 1992 European Championship with Denmark.

"CONCENTRATION AS A GOALKEEPER NEEDS TO BE VERY HIGH. WE WORK ON THE FOCUS IN TRAINING AND IT'S GOOD BECAUSE, IN BIG TEAMS, ONE SAVE... CAN BE DECISIVE."
**THIBAUT COURTOIS**

# CENTRAL DEFENDERS

The defensive rocks in a side, central defenders have to be strong and physical. They must also be tough tacklers and very good in the air to head the ball away and stop an attack.

Top central defenders, like Vincent Kompany, are often rugged and competitive. They must mark the other team's strikers, sticking close to them and not giving them space to turn and attack goal. They are usually the leaders and organisers of the defence.

NUMBERS GAME

**35**

The fee in millions of pounds, Paris St German paid AC Milan to buy Thiago Silva, making him one of the world's most expensive defenders.

VINCENT KOMPANY

*A two-time Premier League winner with Manchester City, Vincent Kompany is a tough, skilled defender. He made his debut for the Belgium national team at the age of just 17 and has since played 60 times for his country.*

# FOOTBALL ICONS

**NAME:** .. FRANZ BECKENBAUER
**NATIONALITY:** .......... GERMAN
**DATE OF BIRTH:** .... 11/09/1945
**INTERNATIONAL CAPS:** ..... 103

Beckenbauer is the only European footballer to win the FIFA World Cup as a player (1974) and manager (1990). He revolutionised defending by moving forwards with the ball, linking defence with attack and scoring more than 90 goals during his long career.

Thiago Silva has won the league championship in both Italy and France and Olympic bronze and silver medals with Brazil.

## THIAGO SILVA

Central defenders don't just stop goals. With their ability to leap high and head the ball powerfully, they can also create and score them. They will often go into the other team's penalty area when their side has a corner or free kick, looking to score. Brazilian central defender, Thiago Silva has scored more than 30 goals for club and country.

"THIAGO SILVA HAS NO RIVAL IN HIS POSITION. HE IS BY FAR THE BEST DEFENDER IN THE WORLD." **LEGENDARY ITALIAN DEFENDER, PAOLO MALDINI**

# FULL BACKS

Full backs are defenders who play closest to the sides of the pitch. They need to be fast to cope with attacks from speedy opposition wingers and strong when tackling.

Full backs used to only worry about defending, but not any more. Top operators like German star, Philipp Lahm, need terrific energy to not only defend but also to race up the pitch to join in their own team's attacks. Lahm is so skilled that he can play on the left or right side of the pitch and in the 2014–15 season, often played in midfield.

PHILIPP LAHM

Philipp Lahm has won the Bundesliga (German League) seven times with Bayern. He has appeared at three FIFA World Cups, helping Germany finish third in 2006 and 2010, and become World Cup winners in 2014.

## FOOTBALL ICONS

NAME: ............ PAOLO MALDINI
NATIONALITY: ............ ITALIAN
DATE OF BIRTH: .... 26/06/1968
INTERNATIONAL CAPS: ..... 124

A one-club man, Paolo Maldini joined the AC Milan youth system before he was a teenager and only retired in 2009 when he was 41. In between, he played more than 900 matches for the club, winning the Champions League five times and the Italian league seven times.

### NUMBERS GAME

## 50

The number of seconds after kick-off that Paolo Maldini scored the Champions League's fastest goal in the final in 2005.

## JORDI ALBA

Jordi Alba has won the Spanish league twice with Barcelona, as well as the Copa del Rey, the Spanish Super Cup and the Champions League. He also won the European Championships with Spain in 2012.

Top full backs are expected to be good at crossing the ball into the penalty area for a teammate to create a scoring chance. In Serge Aurier's first World Cup game for Ivory Coast, against Japan in 2014, two of his crosses resulted in goals for his side.

"YOU CAN PLAY HIM WHEREVER YOU WANT AND HE'LL BE FLAWLESS. HE IS ONE OF THE WORLD'S BEST PLAYERS."
BAYERN MUNICH ASSISTANT COACH HERMANN GERLAND ON PHILLIP LAHM

# UTILITY PLAYERS

Several top footballers play in one position but can, if the coach demands, play in a different one. Certain players are especially versatile and able to play in a number of different positions around the pitch.

Utility players are a valuable part of a team's squad. They allow a coach to make changes more easily if there are injuries or the coach wishes to change tactics. A full back, for example, may be asked to play as a winger if a team needs to add an extra player in attack.

DAVID ALABA

Austria's David Alaba is so versatile that he has been played as a left full back, a right winger and in central midfield. A member of the successful Bayern Munich team that has won three Bundesliga titles and the UEFA Champions League, he also takes a mean free kick.

Javier Mascherano has won two Olympic gold medals (2004, 2008) and has played at three World Cups with Argentina. At the 2014 World Cup, he made more successful tackles than any other player, and completed 515 passes, the third most at the tournament.

Some players are skilled at playing in defence or further forwards. Javier Mascherano plays mostly as a central defender for his club side, Barcelona, but in midfield for Argentina, with whom he reached the final of the 2014 FIFA World Cup.

**JAVIER MASCHERANO**

Happy in midfield or upfront as a striker, Tim Cahill spent eight years with Everton, becoming their second-highest Premier League goalscorer, before moving to New York Red Bulls and, in 2015, Shanghai Shenhua in China.

**TIM CAHILL**

"HE'S A COMPLETE PLAYER... A GUY WHO CAN OPERATE IN SEVERAL POSITIONS, ALL OVER THE PITCH IN FACT."
BAYERN MUNICH COACH, PEP GUARDIOLA ON DAVID ALABA

# MIDFIELDERS

Strong all-round players with great energy, midfielders are expected to both attack and defend. They must work hard for the full 90 minutes to ensure their team has a chance of winning.

Some of a midfielder's work can be unglamorous, but it is still important. It can involve tackling opponents with the ball or sprinting hard to get back into defence. Players like Arturo Vidal are skilled at breaking up opposition attacks as well as starting attacks of their own.

ARTURO VIDAL

FRANK LAMPARD +

The middle of the pitch is often crowded with players, so midfielders need excellent ball control skills to gather and shield the ball from opponents. They must be good at spotting teammates in space and, like German midfielder, Toni Kroos, be able to pass using either foot.

Frank Lampard won four FA Cups and three Premier League titles with Chelsea before moving to Manchester City in 2014. In April 2014, he scored his 250th goal in club football, a remarkable tally for a midfielder. In 2015, he moved to New York City FC.

NUMBERS GAME

# 544

The number of successful passes Toni Kroos made in the 2014 World Cup – more than any other player.

## TONI KROOS

*Real Madrid midfielder, Toni Kroos is a superb passer of the ball. By the age of 24, he had already won the World Cup with Germany and the Champions League with Bayern Munich, with whom he also won three Bundesliga titles.*

*Able to tackle, pass, run with the ball and shoot, sometimes from long distance, Arturo Vidal is a complete midfielder. The Chilean has won four Serie A titles in a row with Juventus (2012–15) and was Juventus player of the year in 2012–13.*

"LAMPARD HAS BEEN UNBELIEVABLE. I DON'T THINK A MIDFIELD PLAYER WILL BE ABLE TO DO THAT FIGURE AGAIN. IT'S QUITE PHENOMENAL."

SIR ALEX FERGUSON ABOUT LAMPARD SCORING MORE THAN 200 GOALS FOR CHELSEA

# MIDDLE OF THE PITCH

Teams play with three, four or five midfielders in a game. They can expect to be involved in the action at both ends of the pitch. Top players in these positions can change games and often produce match-winning performances.

Midfielders can help a team set the tempo (speed) of play and help their team to launch attacks. They may do this by making a powerful run forwards with the ball, passing accurately to teammates or taking a shot themselves. Renowned passer, Andres Iniesta, turned Spanish hero in 2010 when he scored the goal in the final that won Spain the FIFA World Cup.

## KRISTINE LILLY

When it comes to goals scored for a national team, no midfielder can approach the star US women's player, Kristine Lilly. She scored a staggering 130 goals for her national team, winning both the Olympic Games and the Women's World Cup twice each.

Powerful midfielder, Yaya Toure can play almost as an extra defender or he can move forwards to attack. He has scored more than 100 goals. These include scoring the winner in both the semi-final and final of the 2010–11 FA Cup, winning the competition for Manchester City.

**YAYA TOURE**

**ANDRES INIESTA**

The African Footballer of the Year for four years running (2011–14), Yaya Toure has won the league championship in four countries. In 2015, he helped Ivory Coast win their first African Cup of Nations tournament since 1992.

Andres Iniesta is an accurate passer of the ball for Spain and for his club side, Barcelona, with whom he has made almost 600 appearances. He has won the Spanish league six times and the UEFA Champions League three times.

NUMBERS GAME

2,075

The average number of passes Iniesta made per season in La Liga in Spain, three times as many as a typical player.

# WINGERS

Wingers play wide, close to the sidelines of the pitch. There, they can receive the ball and try to beat defenders so that they can cross the ball into the area, pass to a teammate or shoot on goal.

Many wingers, such as Gareth Bale and Arjen Robben, rely on explosive bursts of pace to race past a defender and get into a position to attack. They may push the ball ahead and past the defender and then sprint onto it. Alternatively, they may time a fast run to receive the ball from a teammate.

## NUMBERS GAME

### 36.9

The speed in kilometres per hour that Gareth Bale has run in a match – making him the fastest professional footballer in a top league.

## GARETH BALE

Gareth Bale can run 100 metres in less than 11 seconds and has a blistering shot. In 2013, he was sold for a record fee for a British player when Real Madrid signed him for more than £75 million.

"HE MAKES THINGS LOOK EASY; HIS PACE IS FRIGHTENING. HIS ACCELERATION IS UNBELIEVABLE."

**FORMER WORLD PLAYER OF THE YEAR, ZINEDINE ZIDANE, ABOUT GARETH BALE**

## FRANCK RIBÉRY

Ribéry has played for five different French clubs as well as for Galatasaray in Turkey. With Bayern Munich, he has won the German league four times and the UEFA Champions League once. He has played 81 matches for the French national team, scoring 16 goals.

## ARJEN ROBBEN

Top wingers need a range of skills to compete at the highest level. Some are superb at dribbling where they run with the ball under close control using small nudges of their feet. They may mix this with swerves and stepovers, tricking a defender into thinking they will move one way before moving in another.

Fast, tricky and skilful, Dutch winger, Arjen Robben has won the league championship in four different countries: the Netherlands, England, Spain and Germany. He has scored 28 goals for the Dutch national team.

21

# ATTACKERS

In many teams, one or two players act as a link between strikers and midfielders. These advanced midfielders or attackers link play and the best can be devastating, winning matches for their team.

**EDEN HAZARD**

*Quick and elusive, Eden Hazard has already played more than 50 games for Belgium. His eye for an important pass or goal has made him one of the most sought-after players in Europe.*

Attackers like Eden Hazard are highly skilled footballers who are able to dribble and beat defenders, turn and move in the most crowded of spaces and execute perfect through balls to assist teammates to score. They sometimes help create space for their teammates to run into as well.

By the time he was just 23, the exciting and explosive Neymar was already a league winner in two countries (Brazil and Spain) and a winner of the UEFA Champions League with Barcelona. This gifted attacker with pace and flair has already scored 44 goals for Brazil.

## NEYMAR

Sometimes, attackers are asked to play directly behind a central striker. In this position, they are looking to shoot or help create a scoring chance for someone else. In the 2014–15 season, Raheem Sterling played in this position for Liverpool, but in some matches was asked to play as a winger and even up front as a lone striker.

## MARTA VIEIRA DA SILVA

Marta has won five league championships in Sweden and the USA. She was the player of the tournament at the 2007 Women's World Cup and won FIFA world female player of the year five years in a row.

NUMBERS GAME

95

The number of games Marta has played for Brazil and the number of goals she has scored for her country.

23

# SHOOT OUT!

Cristiano Ronaldo and Lionel Messi are regarded as the two best footballers on the planet. Both have bags of tricks, great skill and an eye for scoring goals, often spectacular ones.

*Since his move to Real Madrid, Christiano Ronaldo has scored more than 300 goals for the Spanish giants at a rate of better than one per game.*

Cristiano Ronaldo scored more than 100 goals for Manchester United. However, on moving to Real Madrid in 2009 for a world record fee (£80 million) he has become even more prolific. Fast, powerful and with a bundle of outrageous tricks and skills, he is one of the most exciting players around.

RONALDO

"HE HAS MAGIC IN HIS BOOTS... HE BELIEVES HE CAN DO ANYTHING WITH THE BALL."
**LEGENDARY PORTUGUESE STRIKER, EUSEBIO ABOUT CRISTIANO RONALDO**

"MESSI IS CLASS. THERE IS HIM, AND THEN THERE IS THE REST. WHAT HE DOES IS EXTRAORDINARY, HE DEMANDS ADMIRATION."
**FRENCH WINGER, FRANCK RIBÉRY**

NUMBERS GAME

**91**

The number of goals in competitive games Lionel Messi scored for Barcelona and Argentina in a single year (2012) – a world record.

MESSI

Lionel Messi moved from his native Argentina to Spain to join Barcelona as a 13 year old and has never left. His dribbling and ball skills make him a defender's nightmare and he once scored in 21 Spanish league games in a row. He has won seven Spanish league titles and four UEFA Champions League crowns with Barcelona.

With an amazing sense for the possibility of a goal, Messi is the all-time top scorer in both the Spanish league and the UEFA Champions League.

# STRIKERS

Strikers are the players most likely to score goals. They play nearest to goal and expect to receive good passes and crosses from teammates. They then try and turn these into scoring chances.

WAYNE ROONEY

Sometimes, more delicate skills are required than a thumping shot or header. A top striker may coolly pass the ball into the net, away from the goalkeeper, rather than strike the ball hard. Or they may choose to pass to a teammate who is in a better position to score or attempt to dribble round the goalkeeper.

England's leading goal scorer scored a hat trick on his Champions League debut for Manchester United back in 2004. Rooney has now scored more than 230 goals for Manchester United with whom he has won the Premier League five times.

**LUIS SUÁREZ**

Strikers obviously need a cool head and an accurate shot. Their reactions must be sharp to get to the ball first and then they need a cool head to pick the right option. Should they shoot first time or take a touch? A world-class striker like Luis Suárez, makes his decision in the blink of an eye.

A striker who can torment opponents with his ball control skills and eye for the unexpected, Luis Suárez has played more than 80 times for Uruguay and scored goals at every club he has played for – a list that includes Ajax, Liverpool and Barcelona.

## FOOTBALL ICONS

NAME: PELÉ (EDSON ARANTES DO NASCIMENTO)

NATIONALITY: ...... BRAZILIAN

DATE OF BIRTH: ... 23/10/1940

INTERNATIONAL CAPS: ....... 92

Pelé scored more than 1,200 goals during his career and is the only player to win three World Cups (1958, 1962, 1970). He could score towering headers, swerving shots or delicate chips over the keeper, as well as make goals for others.

"I SOMETIMES FEEL AS THOUGH FOOTBALL WAS INVENTED FOR THIS MAGICAL PLAYER."
**SIR BOBBY CHARLTON ON PELÉ**

# SCORERS

Strikers are among the most prized players in football, and the most expensive, because of their ability to score goals frequently. They need to be strong mentally as all strikers go through periods when they are unable to score.

Strikers are often closely marked by the other team's defenders, so they have to seek out space or use sharp skills to get to the ball and keep it. Some strikers are tall, strong and especially skilled at winning the ball in the air or holding onto it on the ground.

Robert Lewandowski's goals have helped both Borussia Dortmund and Bayern Munich win the Bundesliga. The Polish striker scored all four goals in Dortmund's 4-1 defeat of Real Madrid in the 2012–13 Champions League – the first time a player has scored four in a semi-final.

ROBERT LEWANDOWSKI

28

Top strikers stay alert until the final whistle. They know that tiring opposition defenders may give them a great chance to score in the dying moments of a game. Sergio Aguero's last-gasp goal in the 94th minute of the last match of the 2011–12 Premier League season won Manchester City their first league title in 44 years.

## NUMBERS GAME

# 15

The age at which Sergio Aguero first played in the top division in Argentina in 2003, breaking a record set by Diego Maradona.

Timing and anticipation along with a rocket of a shot make Sergio Aguero one of the world's most feared strikers. He has won the Europa League with Atlético Madrid, two Premier League titles with Manchester City and an Olympic gold medal with Argentina.

## ABBY WAMBACH

Abby Wambach is a veteran of more than 230 international matches for the US women's team. She has scored a world record 177 goals, more than any other footballer, male or female.

"I'VE NEVER SCORED A GOAL WITHOUT GETTING A PASS FROM SOMEONE ELSE."
ABBY WAMBACH, PAYING TRIBUTE TO TEAMMATES WHO HELPED HER CREATE GOALSCORING CHANCES

# QUIZ

 **1.** In 2012, did Lionel Messi score: 56, 73 or 91 goals?

**2.** Did Toni Kroos, Javier Mascherano or Andres Iniesta make the most successful passes at the 2014 World Cup?

**3.** How many seasons in a row did Cristiano Ronaldo manage to score 50 or more goals for Real Madrid?

**4.** Who scored the winning goal in the 2010 World Cup Final?

**5.** For which country do Eden Hazard, Vincent Kompany and Thibaut Courtois all play?

**6.** Who was awarded the best goalkeeper of the 2015 Women's World Cup?

**7.** For which team did Robert Lewandowski score four goals in a single Champions League semi-final game?

**8.** Which player, male or female, has scored more goals for their national team than any other?

# WEBSITES AND BOOKS

**http://www.fifa.com/**
The official FIFA website is packed full of features, statistics and news.

**www.uefa.com**
The homepage of the Union of European Football Associations, the organisation that runs the European Championship and the Champions League.

**http://news.bbc.co.uk/sport1/hi/football/skills/default.stm**
Enjoy videos of star footballers performing key skills and techniques.

**http://www.football-bible.com/soccer-info/soccer-positions-explained.html**
An interesting article on different playing positions on the pitch.

*Truth or Busted: Football*
by Adam Sutherland (Wayland, 2014)

*Radar Top Jobs: Being a Professional Footballer*
by Sarah Levete (Wayland, 2013)

*Football Joke Book*
by Clive Gifford (Wayland, 2013)

**African Cup of Nations**
Africa's leading competition for national teams from the continent.

**box**
Term used to describe the penalty area on the pitch.

**Bundesliga**
The German league championship competition.

**chip**
A stabbing kick of the ball which sends it steeply upwards often over an opponent or the goalkeeper when trying to score.

**cross**
A pass made from the edges of the pitch into the centre, usually with the ball entering the penalty area.

**distribution**
How a goalkeeper throws or kicks the football after it is under their control.

**dribbling**
Moving the ball under close control using a number of small taps or nudges of the ball.

**FIFA**
Short for the *Fédération Internationale de Football Association*, the organisation that runs world football.

**marking**
To guard an opponent, sticking close to them as they move to deny them time and space to attack.

**penalty shoot out**
A series of penalties taken after the end of a game to decide which team will win.

**possession**
When a player or team keeps control of the

**Serie A**
The top division of t Italian football leagu

**substitution**
When one player lea the game replaced fresh player due to or a change of tacti

**through ball**
An attacking pass played past the oth team's defenders.

# INDEX

The publisher would like to thank the following for their kind permission to reproduce their photographs:
**Key: (t) top; (c) centre; (b) bottom; (l) left; (r) right**
All images **Dreamstime.com** unless otherwise indicated.
7(tr) Dutch National Archives, 9(br) Carlsberg, 11(tr) German Federal Archive, 12(br) P. Eneha,
18(br) Johnmaxmena2, 19(cr) Ailura, 23(bl) Johnmaxmena, 27(br) AFP/SCANPIX, 29(br) Harvardton.